# IMMA FOUNDATION

## LAUNCH OF THE IRISH MUSEUM OF MODERN ART

**Cv/Visual Arts Research Volume 89**

IMMA FOUNDATION
Launch of
The Irish Museum of Modern Art

ISBN 1-904727-44-1
ISSN 1476-9980



This interview was first published in
*Cv Journal of the Arts 4.2*
(London: Cv Publications 1991)

British Library Cataloguing in Publication Data.
A catalogue record of this book is available from the British Library



A digital format publication produced by
Cv Publications, Barley Mow Business Centre,
Barley Mow Passage, London W4 4PH
www.tracksdirectory.ision.co.uk

Cv/VAR Interview
The transcript of the original recording was checked, amended and approved by the featured subject for publication.

## Cv/Visual Arts Research

The survey began in April 1988 as interviews with jewellers, fashion designers and furniture restorers, based at Old Loom House in Whitechapel, launching a quarterly review *Cv Journal of Art and Crafts*. *Cv Journal* was published to 1992 and the collection of interviews, features and reviews provided the foundation of the Cv/Visual Arts Research archive and subsequent publications.

Cv/*VAR* addresses the fields of academic research, galleries and museums worldwide, and a non-specialist readership. The data base is categorized as *Interviews-Artists; Curators and Collections; CraftsDirectory; Small Histories; Social Studies* and *Studio Work.* Titles are published as conventional books and digital files made as print on demand, as well as CDs and DVDs in Cv Publications' software catalogue.

In Cv/VAR 88 IMMA's first director Declan MacGonagle is interviewed by David Rose in 1990 at the launch of the new Irish Museum of Modern Art (IMMA) Dublin. There is an extensive dialogue in which MacGonagle reveals an imaginative approach to curation of art for and within the community, but framed in an international context.

## Contents

# IRISH MUSEUM OF MODERN ART

*Interview with Declan MacGonagle, director of the Irish Museum of Modern Art, Dublin, by David Rose. Recorded in February 1991.*

DR. *Declan MacGonagle, thank you very much for giving me this interview. Can we begin with your relationship with the building, and the new gallery's relationship with the building how you see an old formal building with a heavily loaded history interacting with the concerns and language of 20th century art?*

DMcG. Well I think you have put your finger on it by saying that it is *loaded* with history. Increasingly it is my understanding that those artists that I would find interesting and, I think, have the most to contribute, are those people who are trying to deal with all sorts of loaded histories in different contexts. Obviously the loaded history here is quite specific to the complex relationships with England, indeed with Europe, for in fact the architecture of the building refers to a European tradition as well. I have said right from the beginning, even before I was involved in the project, when it was first mooted and there was a debate in Dublin about the advisability of the RHK building (Royal Hospital a t Kilmainham), against the 19th century warehouse solution in the new docklands financial district; that in setting up a museum from scratch in this country at this time, and to deal with the future questions that we shall face, then such a museum should be located in the context of the neighbourhood where those histories are present and lived through every day. Because that gives us, gives me, an opportunity to make all of that the subject of our work. That would have been much more difficult to do in a state physically disconnected from the community, granted that the other proposal was a 19th century warehouse. But the idea of converted warehouses is a product, of a sort, of New York the result of the process that took over New York in the '60s, where people moved into warehouses for economic reasons, and out of that came this loft style living, and also the use of these economically viable spaces. So it was never God-given that modern art should be contained in these warehouses. It was simply a set of social, political and economic circumstances that created the pattern. I think we may be starting something from scratch here, with the chance to examine the pattern, decide what is useful within it, and either adopt it or move away from it. I think the beauty of the decision here, which may have been made for other reasons, is that it is a fantastic opportunity to set about creating something capable of dealing with both the present and the future, and doing it by using the past, and bringing into play in a contemporary arena all those historical references that, one view would have it, should remain outside art. My view is that is the substance of art, and that's what gives art its value in society. It is absolutely fundamental. I can see this as a container that holds the museum, but we're not simply a tenant in a conveniently maintained building. This building, the fabric of this building, its history, the site, which predates the building in relation to the development of Dublin, are going to be part and parcel of the development of our work.

*I think we will be coming back to aspects of that, because everything we will talk about does come back to that! Originally, when people were discussing the possible venues for IMMA, there was some confusion as whether there was going to be a museum of modern art within the RHK, as you say, a tenant within the building, or whether the RHK was going to be itself that museum. Now clearly you are taking the second sense, but at the same time, as I understand it, conferences and banquets and so forth, will also continue here. I am wondering if there is a certain amount of conflict there, between something that is bound to be marketed (or will it be marketed?) as a superior venue where people can look good. Would certain functions be deemed inappropriate for example?*

*Would you turn them down? What interface will there be between the people who come here on a conference, and the museum itself?*
The starting point is that this whole site will become the museum of modern art. We will refer to it as being at the RHK, because people, taxi drivers, know where that is. Also the reference means that you do conjure up those historical associations and references. The building is a gift on a number of levels the conceptual level, but also the practical level, because it is built round a quadrangle with four wings; with the north wing, in a sense, the most elegant, sort of grandiose. That is where the rooms are that are used for conferences and seminars and banquets, state occasions and so forth. I have walked through them with many artists who have been visiting from outside Ireland to have a look, with the possibility of working in the future. Their reaction has always been that this is a work of art of Ireland.The north wing is already, with the banqueting hall and chapel, a very powerful cultural statement. It contains certain values, it is very clear what it is about. And it is going to be very difficul for artists to engage with that, because it is like engaging with the work of another artist. But the architecture releases us from the problems if we go with it. If we work against it, I think it poses enormous problems.

IMMA FOUNDATION

LAUNCH OF THE IRISH MUSEUM
OF MODFERN ART

*In the context of this building yourself into the fabric, can I raise the subject of the title Gallery or Museum? Are these really different concepts, or is Museum a buzz word, simply because Oxford and New York have museums of modern art?*

I think it was a buzz word, but again I take up this issue of the advantage of the disadvantage. People say to me that it should be *Gallery of Contemporary Art*, for instance, but I think you can invest language with new meaning. Just as new functions are being created for this old building. The word museum in Europe does not carry the meaning of a dead place. In fact, I see it as one of the tasks of the museum, to redefine the word, explore its meaning and history. Neither I as an administrator, nor the building, are transparent mediators. We are making decisions, we are making things happen. And whatever happens doesn't arrive from outer space, with a sort of authoritative glow of museum status around it. And the name does link it to other museums of modern art, a constituency is identified, and the requirement is fulfilled in identifying the national role - the *Irish Museum of Modern Art*. And it does give us the opportunity to counterpoint, say, the Museum of Modern Art in New York, which is a particularly dominant, modernist model of what a museum can and should be in the 20th century, while we are late

**IMMA FOUNDATION**

LAUNCH OF THE IRISH MUSEUM
OF MODFERN ART

world is much more confused, fragmented. So from scratch we can question these earlier models, confounding or contradicting some expectations, complementing others. Nothing should be taken as given, everything should be up for reconsideration.

*Working with living artists extends the view of what is art. You are clearly not going to be the curator of a collection of masterpieces, and leaving it at that.*

We have a number of functions to cover. I do think that we have to demonstrate, right from the start, that we can curate a collection of masterpieces, if that is necessary for the programme, but that we are also capable of generating other readings of those masterpieces, and other readings of what art is, and is for. And we will do that, as you said, by working largely with living artists. So, yes, I don't see myself as a curator of dead objects. I actually think that the art object is simply evidence of the process that has gone on in creating it, and is evidence of the process that can go on when the viewer comes to engage with the work. Now, if we borrow works from another museum, we have to look after them, have lighting controls and so on, but we only really create a critical presence for ourselves, and so be an effective institution, if we operate with a sort of critical momentum.

In other words, we will not borrow from another museum just because of the fame of an artist, but because there is a critical point to be made with those borrowings, and so underpin our whole attitude. To be able to draw upon the widest possible evidence, we need to be capable of operating as a Museum with a capital M, as well as something which questions it. There is a double role; we are establishing a museum, but also questioning one.

*We have other modern galleries in Dublin the Hugh Lane Municipal Gallery, the RHA Gallagher Gallery, the Douglas Hyde. Do you think the presence of the IMMA somehow destabilises them?*

Not at all, I think it actually releases them from a lot of pressure. Again I am a believer in seeing everything as an opportunity. We will be having regular meetings, because I think there is a fantastic opportunity at the moment, which has come about totally fortuitously, that there is a new beginning right across the city *(referring to new appointments at other galleries)*, and there is the regeneration of The National Gallery as well. The sooner we can sit down and say, here is the long term strategy for all artists, examine our critical function in both Ireland and the wider area, the better. We can do that much better together than individually. And I am happy to talk and tell anybody how I am working.

**IMMA FOUNDATION**

LAUNCH OF THE IRISH MUSEUM
OF MODFERN ART

The city will get more if we complement, and we should. The history of museums and galleries has been that people in the main don't believe it's for them. That has been a tragic circumstance for artists to work through, a feeling that a gallery cuts you off from a community. What I would like to do here is to establish this institution as one where the work shown is a way of connecting with the community. This is a very privileged building, a very privileged site, and I am sure there is resistance in an area like Kilmainham to the idea of this building even. I would be very curious to find out how many people have been through the gate from this particular neighbourhood. When people say to me that the museum is very far away from the city centre, my answer is that it is not very far away from Kilmainham. The attitude that describes it as far away implies that art and culture are for people who do not live in Kilmainham. But art, to be of value, must address all sorts of people, and the key to that is diversity of programming; not just in terms of exhibitions, but in terms of the way we mediate those exhibitions. And again, the architecture of this building lends us to that diversity of programming. We can create within the community, rather than imposing a programme. How we sell it to a community is a different thing.

IMMA FOUNDATION

LAUNCH OF THE IRISH MUSEUM
OF MODFERN ART

*I know that you believe that the very concept of regionalism is something that has been invented at the centre. At last year's conference on Regionalism and the Centre at TCD, I did not hear the notion expressed that possibly, instead of centre and regions, or margins, or periphery, what you have is a series of centres, each with its own hinterland. I lived in West Cork for many years, and people said that was remote, but, to take your point, I wasn't remote from the nearest village, and Cork people do not think they are remote from Dublin; they think they are central to Cork. In Skibbereen they don't think they are remote, unless they happen to be in Dundalk! So it moves on down to one homestead, or one lonely farm.*

Absolutely. If I had stayed in Derry, the task would have been, not to have worked with bigger and bigger international names, but to embed the practice further in the community. The function, the process, is the important thing. Regionalism comes out of the 19th century idea of the nation state which created a centre and regions. That's a hierarchical definition that you value the less, the further way you are from the metropolitan centre. All of that is breaking up, it's not where the new thinking is coming from. It is coming from people on the edge, socially or geographically. You can set up a model of something working in a specific locality to the highest possible standards. I am not one who believes in the term or philosophy, *community arts,* because it is a sort of in-built sub-standardisation of work the real thing, and then community art. The true practice is one of enabling and empowering people to make their own decisions and not receive a script from elsewhere.

Regions tend to be administrative areas, but there is a far more vital and important social demarcation of a society that goes on geographically, and politically, and economically. What I'm suggesting is that we engage with that mapping which is people's minds already, that we go right through into the fabric that people understand and live their lives through. That is what we previously engaged with when we were all part of the common currency. The 19th century created the concept of the artist, who is someone disconnected from society, but that notion, and the one of the avant-garde, of the artist being ahead, is one that, now we are coming to the end of the 20th century, can be returned; we can re-establish the idea of locality and the artist (and therefore art), as a product o the social environment. If we operate on that basis, if you unlock that relationship, it is just extraordinary what can actually happen.

*With the Orchard Gallery you deconstructed the idea of the gallery in the Bond Street sense, it couldn't have been further from that. The walls melted and the gallery merged with the city. I know it is called Orchard because it is in Orchard Street, but one does have a rather nice resonance there. But then you had the walls of Derry, it could almost be a construct, or paradigm of engagement with environment. But did you engage with the walls, and do you see scope for that here?*

One of the last things we did before I left was an architectural exhibition. We set out to demonstrate that Derry was not a hole in the ground, but was built in the context of a mainstream European tradition. Comparative studies by students from Queen's showed very clearly that Derry, Dublin and European cities all developed organically, whereas a city like Belfast went from being a village, an organic unit, to being a city overnight, linked with the North of England industrial cities which are now facing enormous problems about identity. I can see Dublin as not being that different from Derry therefore, because of its history. And the contemporary reality is very interesting in terms of the way the city is changing, and how that is merged in the city of Dublin, both negatively and positively. So the principle is no different from me addressing the locality of Derry and doing certain things as a result. What I would suggest here is that we address the principles that underline the development of any community. So yes, that process of melting the walls, which is a very good phrase, could take root here as well. I also believe this building allows us almost to say that the walls are already being somewhat melted, because it is porous. This is a phrase I find myself using more and more; a *porous* museum that allows both a flow in and out, and that is crucial I think, for this particular institution.

*When you were at the ICA in London, you must have had a relationship with the neighbourhood. Was it that the culture perhaps defeated you?*

No, no. One of the things that I learned in Derry was that I'm only as effective as I would like to be in a situation where a number of constituencies have to be addressed. It would have deepened my feeling of effectiveness there if we had had a neighbourhood which would have presented a challenge to the institution, or if it was attempting to be international and local at the same time. It would have been a very interesting challenge. When I went back to Derry, I carried that understanding with me, which meant that I was able to work so that the local and international were not mutually exclusive at all. Personally I found it hard to feel just whom I was addressing at the ICA. That was a curious experience, having come from a very, very particular place, where there was no doubt who were being addressed.

*Set between Buckingham Palace and the Admiralty! Would you like to have been director of the Irish Museum of Modern Art if it had been in the Financial Services Centre?*

No, I wouldn't have been interested.

*I expected that answer. You had room to manoeuvre and develop the programme at the Orchard largely because you were starting from scratch, and so you are here, but the chain of command I suppose is rather different. You would presumably have a board that knows its own mind (insofar as any board knows its own mind), rather more clearly than the City Fathers in Derry?*

Well I should correct you there, because nobody knows or thinks they know their own minds more than the local authority counsellors!

*Let's address this thing of the great national institution. There would presumably be pressure on you, perhaps you would even wish, to generate blockbuster exhibitions, lavish catalogues, that sort of thing. Does that conflict at all, because that addresses itself to a constituency which is very used to that sort of art, to what they call the higher art audience perhaps. Would you still hope to involve the community in this, or would it have to be like renting out the place for functions, rather discreet?*

No, no. I am already negotiating with other institutions for exhibitions or projects that they would be initiating, as I did in the Orchard,

**IMMA FOUNDATION**

LAUNCH OF THE IRISH MUSEUM
OF MODFERN ART

where somebody has created an exhibition, is to work with an artist for that to be remade, recreated, rethought even, in many cases, for the new context. That's the way I am working again. We'll start at a modest level curator, and education and community coordinator. The administrative staff is here already, we will add a few people to that and have security people. We have to develop our own identity and we may find in time that we need to provide more in one area than in another. We have to make sure that the functions that are our tasks are catered for. In time we will be collecting works, we will be collecting projects, so we will need someone who is called the curator to look after this. But hopefully the collection will be unlike any other, and thereupon call on different skills from simply cataloguing dusty objects in a dusty store room. Where someone says, thi object is too precious to go on show, I think you have to question what you are doing having the object. There is a practice which has created in some cases, a situation where the conservation department is only happy if the work is kept in a dark room. There's a balance to be struck.

*They need to remember that today is yesterday's future.*

Absolutely. We have to be saying, what is this for? And what must underline the institutional momentum all the time is, what is the

**IMMA FOUNDATION**

LAUNCH OF THE IRISH MUSEUM
OF MODFERN ART

institution for? And that's a debate, I'm not suggesting a consensus. I hope some of the things we do here will benefit that sort of debate in the context of museum conferences or whatever. We will add to the relationship between forward programming and heritage.

*Would you be happy with charges?*

We have debated this in the last six months, we have debated everything. We won't be charding for general admission. We will charge for special exhibitions, and we will look at it again in several years time and see what the reality is. But I think we are in a very good position because we have other activities that can generate income. I think we will invite donations, but open and free to the public, yes, and for special exhibitions, children would be free, and all sorts of concessions.

*Is disabled access catered for?*

That has been catered for, yes. We have lifts to all floors and ramps to the lifts. And we have bought the entire Gene Lambert exhibition of photographs of people with disabilities, and we will show some of those in our opening exhibition. Early next year we are going to do a major exploration of this issue. Not just disabled artists, but the representation of this. That's something we should be quite aware of.

*Presumably you will not give up the concerts and recitals?*
*We would extend those, in fact, and identify other ways in which the music programme and theatre can be extended, and where it can link with the visual arts programme.*
*With your position as head of a national institution, do you see that you will spend a lot of time being diverted from the primary task by attending international conferences, that sort of thing? How would you see yourself on a spectrum that runs up to say, Sir Roy Strong, or Sir John Pope-Hennessy?*
I wouldn't actually. The only link is the designation as director of the museum. I know the sort of thing you are talking about. I think we actually have different agendas, and that it is simply a coincidence that I am called director of museum, and so are they. Our definitions of director, of museum, of art, of culture, would be very different. So I don't see myself even being on that spectrum. I am an artist first, I am not a curator in the sense of having administrative qualifications, or an art history degree. But I feel that is a major advantage. My experience has shown that the key thing will be developing relationships with living artists. If an artist trusts you and believes in the critical opportunity, things happen. We may buy one work and be given another by the artist. So my training in that sense, and experience, is a great asset.

Where we have to bring in scholarship, we will bring it in, the institution will provide for it. But I hope that my sort of, well, off-centre, or off-mainstream academc, curatorial role will assist this museum to become something that is quite separate and different. Separate is the wrong word - something unique, and therefore something of this time.

*Finally, in Fortnight, in December 1989, you said in an article, that one of the goals of cultural activity should be to try and pose the question, Who are we and what can we be? That was the article called Out of Hibernation. I want to put another question against that What are we, and what can we do?*

I was talking to the Community Relations Council in the North and I was arguing that culture has a fundamental role to play in reconstructing a society (and indeed in society as a whole), and some one asked, what is culture? I replied that it was what people make and what people do. Some of that making and doing will be in ways that everybody understands, and using a language that is directly understood as being art. But also I think, how people lead their lives, that too is cultural. People are already participants in a cultural process, just by being alive and making decisions, and acting upon those decisions. And they are not just consumers of cultural products. It is right to say, What do we do? Once you get down to that level of questioning you construct the reality of political systems, which, in the context of extremism, in Northern Ireland, or in the Middle East, comes to the fundamental of What am I? It is happening in Eastern Europe as well. And what does it mean to say, I am Irish? I come from a sort of Catholic nationalist background, what does it mean? Those are just words. All that can really and properly explored, without damaging other people (and that's a key point), through culture. You can then make artefacts which will contain those values.

---

*The Irish Museum of Modern Art is at the Royal Hospital Kilmainham, Dublin 8, Ireland. Telephone +353-1-6718666. Admission is free, with varied charges for special exhibitions*

*David Rose, a critic and historian, directed an arts centre in West Cork, Ireland, for eighteen years. He is a regular writer in the Cork Citizen, and continues to curate exhibitions*

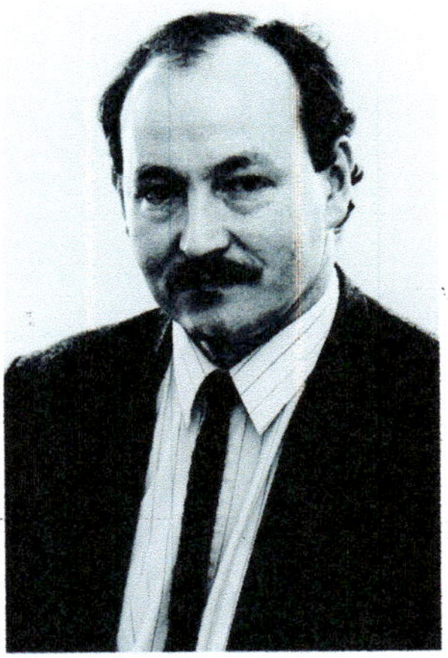

*Other titles from Cv/Visual Arts Research*

Cv/Visual Arts Research Archive

# TATE MODERN

IN CONSTRUCTION

*Other titles from Cv/Visual Arts Research*

**Cv/Visual Arts Research Archive**

# CENTRE DU VERRE

## BOHEMIAN GLASS AT THE MUSÉE DES ARTS DÉCORATIFS

Cv/Visual Arts Research Series 64

# CURATORS & COLLECTIONS

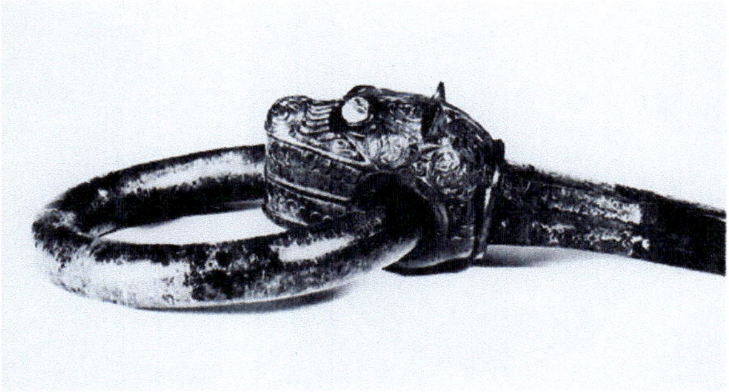

Animal Head with ring. Bronze with glass eyes. Irish 9th Century.
Collection The Nation Museum of Ireland. By permission of The British Museum

Cv: Visual Arts Research Volume 4

**Curators & Collections: Conservation of the Arts** Ed.James/Batiste

ISBN 1-904727-18-2

Book format: A5 size (21 x 14cms), softback, perfect bound with laminated covers.

128 pages, bw ill.. £12.99

**Part 1.** Curators interviews:

CENTRE DU VERRE PARIS *Jean Luc Olivie on Bohemian Glass at Musee Des Arts Decoratifs* ; COURTAULD COLLECTION *John Murdoch on Samuel Courtauld;* IMMA DUBLIN *David Rose & Declan MacGonagle* ; NATIONAL GALLERY *Early Italian Painting + Renoir & The Impressionists* ; TREASURES OF DERRYNAFLAN *Michael Ryan on Early Celtic Metalwork at The British Museum;* ROYAL PHOTOGRAPHIC SOCIETY BATH *Pamela Roberts on Collection of The RPS at Bath* ; THEATRE MUSEUM *Stage Designs and Effects at The Theatre Museum, Covent Garden* ; NATWEST ART COLLECTION Rosemary Harris; DOCUMENTA X, KASSEL *Catherine David In Conference;* TATE MODERN IN CONSTRUCTION *Dawn Austwick & Jeremy Lewison on the new Tate, Bankside*

**Part 2.** Collections Guide, England, Wales and Scotland.